Fact Finders®

IMMIGRATION ★ TODAY

IMMIGRANTS
❦ FROM ❧

INDIA
AND

SOUTHEAST ASIA

BY NEL YOMTOV

CONSULTANT:
S. MITRA KALITA,
JOURNALIST AND AUTHOR OF
*SUBURBAN SAHIBS: THREE FAMILIES
AND THEIR PASSAGE
FROM INDIA TO AMERICA*

CAPSTONE PRESS
a capstone imprint

Fact Finders Books are published by Capstone Press,

1710 Roe Crest Drive, North Mankato, Minnesota 56003

www.mycapstone.com

Library of Congress Cataloging-in-Publication data

Names: Yomtov, Nelson, author.

Title: Immigrants from India and Southeast Asia / by Nel Yomtov.

Description: North Mankato, Minnesota : Capstone Press, 2018. | Series: Fact Finders.

Immigration Today | Audience: Ages 8–10.

Identifiers: LCCN 2018005784 (print) | LCCN 2018007415 (ebook) | ISBN 9781543513820 (library binding) | ISBN 9781543513868 (paperback) | ISBN 9781543513981 (eBook PDF)

Subjects: LCSH: East Indians—United States—Social conditions—Juvenile literature. | Southeast Asians—United States—Social conditions—Juvenile literature. | Immigrants—United States—Social conditions—Juvenile literature. | India—Emigration and Immigration— Social aspects—Juvenile literature. | Southeast Asia—Emigration and Immigration—Social aspects— Juvenile literature. | United States—Emigration and Immigration—Social aspects—Juvenile literature.

Classification: LCC E184.E2 (ebook) | LCC E184.E2 Y66 2018 (print) | DDC 305.9/06912—dc23

LC record available at https://lccn.loc.gov/2018005784

Editorial Credits

Editor: Jennifer Huston

Production Artist: Kazuko Collins

Designer: Russell Griesmer

Media Researcher: Eric Gohl

Production specialist: Laura Manthe

Photo Credits: Alamy: Ethel Wolvovitz, 14; AP Photo: 8, Rogelio V. Solis, 19, The Florida Times-Union/Will Dickey, 27; Getty Images: Dirck Halstead, 9, Hindustan Times, 12, Robert Nickelsberg, 22, 24, 26, T.C. Malhotra, 20, Thierry Falise, 21, 25, Viviane Moos, 11, Yvan Cohen, 23; iStockphoto: FatCamera, 16; Newscom: Liszt Collection, 5; Shutterstock: Aman Ahmed Khan, cover, bioraven, throughout (passport stamps background), dikobraziy, cover (background), 1, Intellistudies, 15, PSboom, 7

Design Elements: Shutterstock

Source Notes: pp. 14, 15, 16: From author's interview with Kanchan Dadarkar, December 4, 2017.

TABLE OF CONTENTS

CHAPTER 1

Indian and Southeast Asian Americans

4

CHAPTER 2

On the Move

10

CHAPTER 3

Immigrants vs. Refugees

18

CHAPTER 4

A "New and Happy Place"

26

Glossary 30

Read More 31

Internet Sites 31

Critical Thinking Questions 31

Index 32

★

INDIAN AND SOUTHEAST ASIAN AMERICANS

Can you imagine leaving behind everything you know to live in a new country? Think about the challenges you would face. You would have to find a new place to live and make new friends. Your parents would need to find new jobs. You might even have to learn a new language. These are the challenges that many **immigrants** experience.

Thousands of immigrants from India and Southeast Asia move to the United States each year. India is a country located in southern Asia. It is slightly more than one-third the size of the United States. With roughly 1.3 billion residents, India is one of the world's most populated countries, second only to China.

A few hundred immigrants from India first came to the United States in the early 19th century. But the Immigration Act of 1924 set limits on immigration based on race and country of origin. During this time, most people from Asia, including those from India, were banned from moving to the United States.

The first Indian immigrants to the United States were farm workers. By the end of the 1800s, around 2,000 Indians had moved to the United States.

 immigrant—a person who moves from one country to live permanently in another

The Immigration and Nationality Act of 1965 got rid of those limits. At the time, there were fewer than 50,000 Indian Americans in the United States. Today around 2.5 million people of Indian origin live in the United States.

The region known as Southeast Asia is located east of India and south of China. Southeast Asia is made up of many nations, including Vietnam, Laos, Cambodia, Burma, Malaysia, Indonesia, and the Philippines.

For many years, few people from Southeast Asia moved to the United States. But during the 1970s, immigration from Southeast Asia increased sharply. Today most of the Southeast Asians living in America are from the Philippines and Vietnam.

★ WHY LEAVE HOME? ★

People move to the United States for different reasons. Since the mid-1990s, many people from India and Southeast Asia have moved to the United States for jobs or school. Indian immigrants are often well-educated professionals, such as doctors, engineers, and computer specialists. Most believe that the chances for success in their careers is better here. Many immigrants also leave to join family members already living in the United States.

INDIA AND SOUTHEAST ASIA

CHINA

BHUTAN

NEPAL

BANGLADESH

INDIA

BURMA

VIETNAM

THAILAND

LAOS

CAMBODIA

PHILIPPINES

BRUNEI

MALAYSIA

SRI LANKA

PACIFIC OCEAN

SINGAPORE

INDONESIA

EAST TIMOR

INDIAN OCEAN

AUSTRALIA

China and Australia shown for context only.
They are not part of Southeast Asia.

Some people leave their home countries to escape political or religious **persecution**. Others are fleeing violence and war. People who have been forced to leave their home countries because of war, persecution, or natural disasters are called **refugees**.

In the 1970s and 1980s, thousands of refugees from Vietnam, Laos, and Cambodia came to the United States. They came to escape **communist** governments and war.

People from South Vietnam watch as their village is bombed during the Vietnam War.

Vietnamese Refugees

Vietnam is a country located in Southeast Asia. In 1975 the United States withdrew from the Vietnam War (1954–1975). But the fighting continued between China and Vietnam. Over the next 20 years, about 1.6 million Vietnamese people left the country to escape the continued fighting and violence. Many of these people fled their homeland in simple boats. They risked their lives to go to another country.

Many Vietnamese refugees resettled in the United States. In 1980 there were about 231,000 Vietnamese-born people living in the United States. By 2016 that number had risen to nearly 1.4 million.

persecution—cruel or unfair treatment, often because of race or religious beliefs

refugee—a person who is forced to leave his or her country to escape war or religious persecution

communist—a form of government where all the land, property, businesses, and resources belong to the government, and the profits are shared by all

ON THE MOVE

During the 1980s, about 30,000 people moved from India to the United States each year. Kanchan Dadarkar and her family were among those immigrants. Leaving behind a comfortable life in India, the Dadarkars traveled to America.

In 1983 Kanchan and her family lived in Mumbai, one of India's largest cities. More than 8 million people were living there at the time. Kanchan and her husband, Anil, had two daughters, ages 5 and 6.

Anil's sister and her family were already living in Queens, near New York City. She often told Anil how nice life was in America. She encouraged him to move to the United States.

Anil decided to move his family to America where they would live with his sister in Queens. Anil was a successful architect in India, but he wanted his family to experience a different kind of life. Kanchan says she felt no strong emotions about leaving her homeland at the time. But soon, that would change.

A crowd gathers at a marketplace in Mumbai, India. Today the city and the surrounding area are home to around 22 million people.

★ THE NEW LIFE BEGINS ★

The Dadarkars' immigration process went smoothly. After waiting several months, the family received their immigration **visas** from the U.S. government. The Dadarkars boarded a plane in Mumbai and flew directly to New York. It was the first airplane trip for everyone. Anil's sister and family greeted the new arrivals at the airport.

Scenes like this occur in airports across the United States when immigrants join loved ones already living in the country.

Anil did not have a job when the Dadarkars arrived in New York. But Kanchan was not worried about the family's money. As in India, her job was to care for the children. Anil took care of the money.

Anil's brother-in-law was an engineer. Within a few weeks, he helped Anil find part-time work. Six weeks later, Anil got a full-time job as an architect. Having worked with Americans at his job in India, Anil spoke English very well. After working a couple of months, the Dadarkars had saved enough money to get their own apartment in Queens.

 visa—a document giving a person permission to enter a foreign country

Thanks to fellow Indian Americans in her neighborhood, Kanchan Dadarkar learned English and felt at ease in her new country.

Kanchan spoke very little English. Although she had studied the language in school, she admits that she "was not very good." Today Kanchan speaks perfect English. She learned a lot of the language by watching TV shows. Kanchan also learned some English from other Indian American women she met in Queens. A large part of the Dadarkars' positive experience was because many fellow Indian Americans lived in their neighborhood.

Over time Kanchan began to work out of her home. First she worked as a babysitter. Then she used her sewing skills to earn money. People hired her to make items that they would sell in stores.

FAR FROM HOME

After living in the United States for two years, Kanchan received news that her brother in India was getting married. That's when she realized how different her life had become. "It hit me," she said. "I'm so far away from everybody." For the first time since Kanchan arrived in the United States, she felt sad about leaving her family in India.

Like Kanchan, many Indian American women use their sewing skills to make traditional Indian clothing and other items.

It was a difficult time for Kanchan, but she continued her work. In 1987 she got a full-time job at a home security company. She enjoyed her work so much that she has remained with the company for more than 30 years.

Kanchan's children are now grown women who live and work in New York. They do not remember much about their lives in India. For them, life in the United States is the only life they've known.

Kanchan has no regrets about moving to the United States. "I feel very happy I got a chance to come here," she said. "Back home, I'd still be a housewife. [Here,] I'm a working woman, and I have confidence in myself. The self-confidence I got here would not happen in India. I became a different person."

Indian Americans are among the most highly educated immigrants in the country, with 70 percent earning a college degree.

NUMBER OF PEOPLE FROM INDIA LIVING IN THE UNITED STATES

Indians are moving to the United States in record numbers. In 2017 the largest group of immigrants coming to the United States was from India. About 54 percent of these immigrants live in California, New Jersey, Texas, New York, and Illinois.

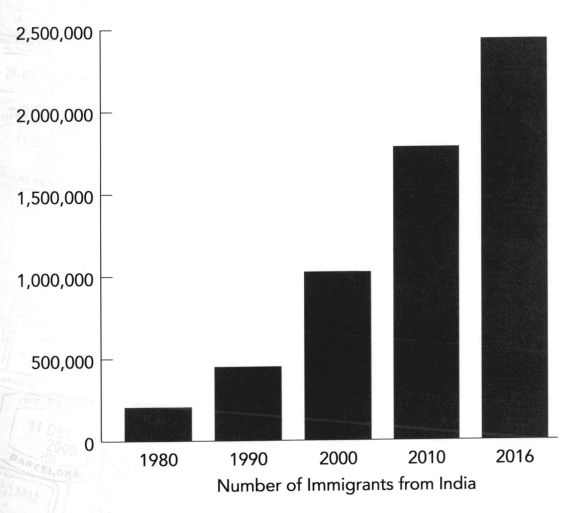

Number of Immigrants from India

Source: Migration Policy Institute

CHAPTER 3

IMMIGRANTS VS. REFUGEES

The U.S. government has different rules for entering the country as a refugee or an immigrant. The government defines refugees as people "who are not able to safely and voluntarily return home. . . ." Refugees are in danger because of their religion, political beliefs, or race. They might also be part of a social group that is being persecuted. Or they could be in need of special medical care. The application process for refugees can take up to two years. Those granted refugee status are given special permission to enter the United States.

Immigrants who want to move to the United States must apply for a visa. The application process can take many years. They have to say why they want to immigrate and list the skills they have. They must also know someone already living in the United States who is willing to **sponsor** them. A sponsor could be a family member or employer.

Both refugees and immigrants can only live in the United States temporarily. If they want to stay, they must apply to become permanent residents. After that they can apply to become U.S. citizens.

A group of immigrants takes the oath of **allegiance** at a ceremony to become U.S. citizens.

sponsor—to be responsible for

allegiance—loyalty and obedience owed to one's country or government

★ A LUCKY FAMILY? ★

For many immigrants, like Hai Blu (pronounced *hey blue*), resettling in the United States is a long and difficult process. Hai Blu's name means "Brings Luck" in Burmese, and it's very appropriate. He's one of millions of immigrants who needed a lot of good fortune to make it to the United States.

Hai Blu belongs to the Karen ethnic group of southern Burma, which is also known as Myanmar. For more than 50 years, the country was ruled by a **military dictatorship** that had all the power. Certain groups, such as the Karen, faced punishment and harsh treatment from the government.

The Burmese people protested the military dictatorship. They even elected a democratic leader, Aung San Suu Kyi (pictured on poster), but the military government arrested her.

The Karen National Liberation Army prepares to fight the Burmese Army.

In 1988 Karen fighters went to war against the Burmese military dictatorship. To escape the violence, Hai Blu's parents fled to a refugee camp in northwestern Thailand. Hai Blu was born in the camp and spent his entire childhood there. Food was scarce and living conditions were poor. Children received little education.

military dictatorship—a type of government where the nation's armed forces are in charge

After living in the refugee camp for more than 23 years, Hai Blu applied for refugee status. In early 2008 the United Nations High Commissioner for Refugees (UNHCR) granted Hai Blu and his family refugee status. This allowed them to resettle outside the camp. For Hai Blu, his wife True Tender, and their 5-year-old son, the United States was to become their new home. In April 2008 they became the first Burmese family to resettle in Burlington, Vermont. For decades, many communities in Vermont have welcomed refugees from around the world.

People from the Vermont Refugee and Resettlement Program helped this family start over in Burlington.

LIFE IN A REFUGEE CAMP

Hundreds of thousands of Burmese refugees spend years living in camps in Thailand, India, and Malaysia. In the refugee camps, there is often not enough food to eat. The refugees are usually not allowed to leave the camp, even to work and earn money.

Burmese refugees line up to receive a meal.

Hai Blu and his family arrived at the Burlington airport late at night. Workers from the Vermont Refugee and Resettlement Program (VRRP) met them there. This organization helps new refugees find housing and get settled in Vermont. The agency also arranges for a small cash allowance, health care, and English lessons, among other basics.

★ A FAMILY'S WORRIES ★

Life in America was safer and more secure than in the refugee camp, but Hai Blu was worried. True Tender was sad about leaving her friends and family behind. She often cried. There were financial worries too. The money they received from the VRRP was barely enough to pay rent on their apartment. Because he did not speak English, Hai Blu worried about getting a job and providing food for his family.

Immigrants and refugees in the United States are often forced to take low-paying jobs. This man does housekeeping duties at a hotel.

With the assistance of the VRRP, Hai Blu found a temporary job at a factory. But to get to work on time, he had to leave the apartment at 5 a.m. Then he didn't return home until late at night. After three months, the temporary job ended, and Hai Blu was once again without a job.

BURMESE CHRISTIANS

In 2017 Christians from Burma made up the largest group of refugees entering the United States. From 2007 to 2016, 25 percent of all refugees going to America were Burmese of all religions and ethnicities. During that time, roughly 160,000 people from Burma moved to the United States.

Burmese Christians practice their faith at a refugee camp.

A "NEW AND HAPPY PLACE"

Although he felt disappointed and frustrated, Hai Blu looked for another job. Eventually, he was hired as a dishwasher at a restaurant. Hai Blu's new boss liked his enthusiasm and good work habits. Over time Hai Blu's English improved, and he received several promotions, each job better than the one before.

An immigrant from Southeast Asia works on an English lesson.

Burmese refugees in Florida attend a class on U.S. citizenship.

Hai Blu was eventually able to buy a car for his family. In their spare time, he and True Tender studied together for their U.S. citizenship tests. The test requires people to fill out an application and answer questions about their background. They're also required to pass an English test and a test about the history of the United States and the functions of the U.S. government.

The Dadarkars and Hai Blu's family both had positive experiences coming to the United States. They faced challenges along the way, but they persisted. Many immigrants are not as lucky. Some face **prejudice** and **discrimination**. Sometimes immigrant students don't receive the help they need, especially if they don't speak English well. Others are bullied and teased because they are immigrants. But many schools in the United States now offer programs to help immigrants learn English. Other programs teach students to respect each others' differences and speak out against prejudice and discrimination.

Hai Blu and his family are grateful for the opportunity to live in the United States. They worked hard to have a good life for themselves. Soon after arriving in Burlington, the couple's second son was born. They named him Lawmu Kaawthaw, which means "New and Happy Place." It reveals how his parents feel about living in the United States.

prejudice—hatred or dislike of people who belong to a certain social group, such as a race or religion
discrimination—treating people unfairly because of their race, country of birth, or gender

NUMBER OF PEOPLE LIVING IN THE UNITED STATES FROM SOUTHEAST ASIA

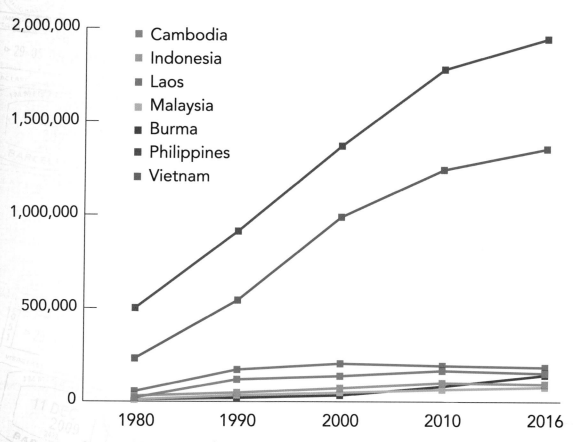

Source: Migration Policy Institute

GLOSSARY

allegiance (uh-LEE-juhnts)—loyalty and obedience owed to one's country or government

communist (KAHM-yuh-nihst)—a form of government where all the land, property, businesses, and resources belong to the government, and the profits are shared by all

discrimination (dis-kri-muh-NAY-shuhn)—treating people unfairly because of their race, country of birth, or gender

immigrant (IM-i-gruhnt)—a person who moves from one country to live permanently in another

military dictatorship (MIL-uh-ter-ee DIK-tay-tur-ship)—a type of government where the nation's armed forces are in charge

persecution (pur-suh-KYOO-shuhn)—cruel or unfair treatment, often because of race or religious beliefs

prejudice (PREJ-uh-diss)—hatred or dislike of people who belong to a certain social group, such as a race or religion

refugee (ref-yoo-JEE)—a person who is forced to leave his or her country to escape war or religious persecution

sponsor (SPON-sur)—to be responsible for

visa (VEE-zuh)—a document giving a person permission to enter a foreign country

READ MORE

Creager, Ellen. *Life as an Indian American.* One Nation for All: Immigrants in the United States. New York, PowerKids Press, 2018.

Jeffries, Joyce. *Who Are Refugees?* What's the Issue? New York: KidHaven Publishing, 2018.

Rodger, Ellen. *A Refugee's Journey from Myanmar.* Leaving My Homeland. New York: Crabtree Publishing, 2018.

Skrypuch, Marsha Forchuk. *Adrift at Sea: A Vietnamese Boy's Story of Survival.* Toronto, Canada: Pajama Press, 2016.

INTERNET SITES

Use FactHound to find Internet sites related to this book.

Visit www.facthound.com

Just type in 9781543513820 and go.

 Check out projects, games and lots more at
www.capstonekids.com

CRITICAL THINKING QUESTIONS

1. What opportunities or features about the United States make it a popular place for immigrants to settle?

2. Imagine you moved to the United States and didn't speak English. What challenges would you face in school and in your neighborhood? How would you want to be treated by your classmates and community?

3. Study the infographic on page 29. Use details from the text and your own knowledge to explain why the Vietnamese population has increased so much since 1980.

INDEX

Blu, Hai, and family, 20–28
Burlington, Vermont, 22, 23
Burma, 6, 20
Burmese military dictatorship, 20–21

challenges immigrants face, 4, 28
  bullying, 28
  homesickness, 15, 24
  housing, 4
  jobs, 4, 13, 14, 24, 25
  language, 4, 14, 24, 28
  prejudice and discrimination, 28
communism, 8

Dadarkar, Kanchan, and family, 10, 12–16, 28

ethnic groups, 25
  Karen, 20

history of U.S. immigration from India, 4, 6, 10
history of U.S. immigration from Southeast Asia, 6

immigrant vs. refugee, 18
Immigration Act of 1924, 4
Immigration and Nationality Act of 1965, 6

Mumbai, India, 10, 12
Myanmar. See Burma

Native Americans, 29

path to U.S. citizenship, 27
Pilgrims, 29

reasons to immigrate, 6
  jobs, 6
  natural disasters, 8
  political persecution, 8
  religious persecution, 8
  reuniting with family, 6
  school, 6
  war, 8
refugee camps, 21, 22, 23
refugees
  Burma, 21–25
  Cambodia, 8
  Laos, 8
  Vietnam, 8, 9
religious groups
  Burmese Christians, 25

successes, 13, 14, 16, 26, 27, 28

Thailand, 21, 23

United Nations High Commissioner for Refugees (UNHCR), 22
U.S. immigration process, 12, 18
U.S. refugee process, 18

Vermont Refugee and Resettlement Program (VRRP), 23, 24, 25
Vietnam War, 9
visa, 12, 18